Meditation

How To Meditate For Beginners: A Guide To Relieving
Stress, Getting Over Anxiety, And Conquering Depression
With Simple, Straightforward Meditation Techniques
That Are Easy To Understand

(What You Can Do To Ease Your Stress And Anxiety)

Marcus Leitgeb

TABLE OF CONTENT

Introduction 1

Known As "Svadhisthana" The Sacral Chakra, Sometimes Referred To As The Naval 8

The Throat Chakra Is Responsible For Communication And For Being Heard. 12

The Significance Of The Chakras 23

Methods Of Breathing That Will Assist You In Keeping Your Chakras Open 26

A Sacral Chakra That Is Both Open And Balanced 32

The Seven Chakras 49

Third Method: Praying 59

The Third Chakra, Located In The Throat. 64

The Soul Star Chakra 71

Symptoms That Your Chakras Are Unbalanced As A Warnng To You 74

The Sacral Chakra 78

Indicators And Problems Caused By An Unbalanced Root Chakra 83

When And Where Exactly Did The Chakras First Appear? 92

The Sacral Chakra Is Located In The Lower Abdomen. 146

Introduction

However, what exactly are chakras? Because of the way energy travels through the body, a Sanskrit word that translates to "wheel" may be used to refer to a chakra. Since we are talking about the body at the moment, please allow me to expand on the topic. Because of their resemblance to spinning wheels, the energy centers of the organization, which make up the bulk of the organization's structure, are often referred to as chakras. These energy centers, or chakras, are responsible for the flow of energy, which may go from one zone to the next after beginning in one zone. These energy centers, known as chakras, are inextricably linked to the day-to-day routine of living because of the strong connections that may be formed between sound, color, and light. In the process of healing, the goal is to balance the chakras by successfully altering them while also focusing on the crucial task of comprehending nature for what it is worth about creation and the function of the individuals in view.

The human body is structured to have a total of seven energy centers known as chakras. The main chakra, also known as the red chakra, is positioned exactly at the base of the spine. It is sometimes referred to as the root chakra because of its proximity to the base of the spine. The Kundalini chakra is another term for this particular chakra. The orange hue represents the second chakra, which is the spleen, and it is located just below the scar left by the umbilical cord. This chakra is the second of the seven chakras. The chakras become more active as a result of meditating, which indicates that the goal of balancing the chakras in order to reach the desired arrangement cannot be accomplished without the practice of meditation. Regardless of this, the second chakra is in charge of determining sexual boundaries, and if it becomes imbalanced, there is room for blame.

The sun-oriented plexus chakra, which represents the seat of emotions and is the source of the yellow hue, is the third of the seven chakras. The color yellow is associated with this chakra and represents authority on earth. The color green represents the fourth chakra, which is also known as the heart chakra. This chakra is seen or manifested when there is a lack of empathy in the spirit, and it is referred to as the heart chakra. This emoji demonstrates the freedom to express one's mind when practicing meditation. The throat chakra is associated with the color blue and is also known as the fifth chakra. The third eye chakra, which is the sixth chakra before we combine them all together to form the seven chakras, is symbolized by the color blue and always features the forehead as a vital component of these energy components.

The crown chakra is the seventh and last chakra, and its mission is to link you with higher realms. It is represented by the color purple, and it is the chakra that concludes the negotiations on the other seven chakras. Chakras are continually visible in the body because they are always absorbing energy while simultaneously increasing with color, light, and sound. Prana is the name given to the deep energy that flows forth from each of these chakras. Prana is absorbed by the chakra centers, which causes them to vibrate, ultimately leading to the delivery of power. When prana merges with the brain, we can say that the fundamental goal of reducing the effects of imbalance in the chakras has been accomplished. This is because prana has joined forces with the brain.

The astral body and the physical body are joined together via a link known as prana. Numerous questions about chakras may be answered via the practice of meditation. For instance, how does the energy first come into being, how does it move, and what are the advantages of doing so? If you have a genuine understanding of the advantages of yoga asana, then you are aware that balancing the chakras provides an additional opportunity for releasing the unstable energy that may cause people to misjudge each other's measurements of the actual world. This has, the majority of the time, been made clear in the course of astral explorations and astral investigations. The following is a list of the terminological words that are used to refer to the seven chakras: Mooladhara, Swadhisthana, Manipura,

Anahata, Vishuddhi, Ajna, and Sahasrara. The purpose of these chakras is to reflect an individual's psychological condition and interpret it in relation to each energy center. Chakras may only be said to be in a condition of fundamental equilibrium if they are allowed to contract their vibration at a predetermined frequency. So, when their energy cannot flow, what do chakras become? When one of the chakras or energy centers is blocked, it has an effect on our physical welfare, which is why people start becoming sick when this happens.

At the end of the day, the energy centers that are the recovering states of these viewpoints are what we call energy centers. In traditional Hinduism, the energy centers, known as chakras in this context, are depicted in several forms of tantric teachings. These works are considered to be authoritative. However, in today's modern world, this idea is related with prana, and its origins may be traced back to the seventeenth century, when a well-known scientist used animal magnetism as a treatment for a particular illness. In any case, there is not yet any academic study done on this marvel despite the fact that the idea of chakras became inextricably linked with the achievements of this doctor.

Known As "Svadhisthana" The Sacral Chakra, Sometimes Referred To As The Naval

The capacity of a person to taste is related to this chakra, which is associated with the element of water. It might be located in the region between the vaginal organs and the sacral plexus nerve. This chakra is concerned with emotions, creative expression, and the satisfaction gained from satisfying personal interactions. It exercises control over the gallbladder and liver, in addition to the stomach, kidneys, and adrenal glands. Lower back discomfort, issues with digestion, problems with the menstrual cycle, hormonal imbalances, pelvic pain, sensations of being fatigued, and problems with psychological worries such as money, power, and a lack of creativity are all symptoms of an imbalance in this chakra. Those who have achieved harmony in this chakra are able to empathize with others, are at ease with their sexuality, enjoy financial success, and have a sense of humor. Amber and orange tourmaline are two types of gemstones that are associated with this chakra. Sandalwood and ylang-ylang essential fragrances are also associated with this chakra.

This chakra is in charge of your physical, mental, and emotional health and well-being. When there is an imbalance in the sacral region, a multitude of different problems may present themselves. These problems may include infertility concerns, phobias of change, and even difficulties in developing close relationships with other people. Whenever there is a weakness in this area, there is sometimes a manifestation of highly emotional behavior. You may strengthen the sacral chakra by practicing even the most basic kinds of yoga. You may find assistance in this area by engaging in a number of yoga positions, and in most cases, all that is required is a little of light stretching to bring about the desired effect of amplifying strong feelings. In this respect, activities such as yoga, listening to music, and engaging in aromatherapy may all be therapeutic.

The chakra is located below the navel in the lower abdomen, and it is responsible for the regulation of the sexual organs, the gonad gland, the liver, the stomach, the gall bladder, the kidney, the upper intestine, the adrenal glands, and the middle spine. It has a significant impact on jubilation, excitement, reproduction, and inventiveness.

difficulties with anger, apathy, hostility, menace, greed, guilt, control, power, immortality, pelvic discomfort, gynecological difficulties, urinary problems, and libido might result from an imbalance in this chakra.

Your Swadhisthana serves as your primary creative hub. It has an impact on your personal authority, wealth, and sexual core, among other areas. This energy point is the conduit via which you may communicate with your inner child, as well as your emotions and sensualities. It is connected to the sensual bodily experiences of love, passion, and sexuality. Additionally, the acts of giving and receiving are made easier by this chakra.

The Throat Chakra Is Responsible For Communication And For Being Heard.

The fifth chakra, often known as the neck chakra, is sometimes referred to by its Sanskrit name, "Vishuddha," which literally translates to "pure." This chakra is associated with our capacity for communication and enables us to give expression to our innermost beliefs. The inspiration, sincerity, intellect, and creativity that come from this chakra are channeled via the throat. It is about expressing our truth and our purpose in life, which is a fundamental way of expression and communication in our culture.

The throat chakra is an etheric energy center that links humans to the spirit world. It sits in the exact middle of the neck and is perpendicular to the trachea (windpipe). Because of its position at the neck, it is often seen of as the "bottleneck" that restricts the flow of energy throughout the body. When we open the throat chakra, we are able to better connect our vision with reality and release the pressure that might potentially have a detrimental effect on the heart chakra, which is located below it.

The color blue (also known as aquamarine or turquoise) is used to symbolize this chakra. A crescent with a circle contained inside it forms part of its symbol, which also has a circle within a circle. It is often shown as a circle inside of which is carved a triangle pointing in a downward direction. This triangle is contained inside another circle.

It is necessary to let go of our denial and the falsehoods that we tell ourselves in order to bring the throat chakra back into equilibrium. Our subconcious mind is able to see right through whatever justification or explanation we provide. It is not possible for us to deceive either ourselves or the outside world on the essence of who we really are.

The Throat Chakra and Different Alternative Methods of Healing

Blue is the color.

Ether, the Element

Position: in the neck, in the hollow right between the shoulder blades

Ailments of the Emotions Caused by Blockages: A propensity to be manipulative, feelings of shyness or discomfort, saying things you may come to regret, a lack of inspiration, and feeling uninspired.

Ailments of the Physical Body Caused by Blockages: Throat discomfort, an overactive or underactive thyroid, as well as pain in the neck or shoulders

Crystals that are used for healing include: turquoise, rainbow fluorite, Ceylon sapphire, blue chalcedony, blue calcite, azurite, aquamarine, lapis lazuli, and topaz.

Coltsfoot, peppermint, and sage are some of the medicinal herbs that may be used.

Agrimony, Cerato, and Mimulus may be used for healing with Bach Flower Therapy.

Camphor, eucalyptus, ginger, and peppermint are some of the essential oils that may be used for healing.

Using sound to heal: chant the "HAM" sound, which is the universal seed sound.

Affirmations may be used to facilitate healing: "I speak my truth lovingly and effortlessly." "I let my truth be my guide, and I speak from the heart."

Initiating the Opening of the Throat Chakra: Begin keeping a diary, make time to sing, muster the bravery to discover your own beliefs, and favor the color blue in your wardrobe.

Meditation and Yoga Position: Neck Rolls while Practicing Lion's Breath

Tantra and Yoga in Their Conceptual Forms

When it first arrived in the 10th century, Tantra completely transformed how yoga was conceived of and practiced. It was a methodical approach to life that is similar to the way Hinduism and Buddhism see the world and how it should be lived. It is the study as well as the practice of the manner in which the body is able to let the prana to go through you and the manner in which you will be able to notice all of the motions that it makes. The term "kundalini" refers to both the movement of the energy and the course that it follows, and it illustrates the many ways in which one's own consciousness might become one with the awareness of the universe.

Tantra is the practice of bringing the energy up in the body from one chakra to the next and activating them in such a way that would enable the individual to be perfectly connected and linked into the cosmos. This is done via a series of yoga postures and breathing exercises.

The skill of activating the chakras, including both its usage and its practice, was kept a secret and was taught in a variety of secluded locales such that only a very small number of individuals were aware of how to do the activation procedure. It is known that there were secret cults that existed in literature as far back as the sixth century BC. These cults practiced their religion in isolated areas so that they would not be disturbed by the forces that came from the outside world.

A Definition of the Charkas

When a chakra is activated, it enables the meditator to gain a new degree of consciousness as well as a new level of being linked into the cosmos. Sometimes, they have been likened to a lotus rather than a wheel. The chakras may be broken down into these fundamental components.

The MuladharaChakra, sometimes called the Root Chakra:

Our physical, vital, and ancestral roots are all contained inside the first chakra. It is situated at the bottom of the coccyx, in the space between the anus and the genitals, and its role in the body is connected to the robustness of the bones, teeth, and nails, as well as the intestinal tract, legs, and feet. It is the energy that is responsible for the development of the other chakras, but this has a psychological, bodily, and emotional expression as well. This is because the Muladhara chakra is the energy center that is responsible for supplying us with our vital energy. Because Sushumna, Ida, and Pingala, the three primary energy channels, all begin at this place, the first chakra is the hub of the cycles of subtle energy medicine. The kundalini is the cosmic energy that speaks the tantric tradition.

Because it is our most fundamental being and its relationship to the ground, as a supplier of life, strength, and protection, this chakra is the one that is most closely aligned with our animal and tribal nature. It is also the one that is furthest distant from our transcendent being. However, it is just as lovely as the things that are more spiritual. It is also the drive that wants our survival, which drives us to act, but also provides us the fundamental fire to work every day. Both of these things are caused by the drive. It is not simply as a primal rhythm, but rather it is exhibited via confidence and warmth body-mind from where the potential for action, creativity, self-esteem, and fundamental drive show off. It is a significant component that enables us to establish our roots, construct, and look for stability.

Because momentum is what gives us life as well as ontological security, confidence, and power, it is a vital component of our existence and relates to an important component of our welfare. This energy refers to our physical state, which includes being linked with the land and the natural surroundings as well as with our body as a manifestation of the earth and listening to their need.

The red that identifies the same hue as the most fundamental energy of the planet, and consequently also of the life that emerges from it. Additionally, the hue of blood comes to mind. The sensation of being protected, having access to food and clothes, and having one's well-being ensured are all things that our instinctual plane of the first chakra need. It is the group root that provides us with a feeling of belonging and a psychological location, and it also contains a map of mental and emotional protection. These are some of the characteristics that this has in addition to the physical one. But if we look at it from a physical standpoint, we see that this being is also connected to natural cycles and the requirements that the body must fulfill in order to grow its potential and its vitality.

The Significance Of The Chakras

Each of the seven chakras has a bundle of nerves, which are essential to our physical, mental, and emotional health. Chakras are located at certain points along the spine. Because of this, the chakras are an essential component of our health and the way in which we are able to experience life. Our chakras need to be correctly aligned, open, and flexible in order to enable the energy to flow easily through our bodies. This is because the energy is always in motion, and because of this, the energy must be able to move freely through our bodies. Permit me to illustrate this point by referring to the bathtub that is located in your master bathroom. If you clean it too often, the hair may accumulate in the drain, causing water to pool in the tub and encouraging the development of mildew, fungus, and viruses. This might happen if you clean it too frequently. This is the exact way that our body functions, with the exception that the chakras are not physically present in the same way that your bathtub's drain is, and thus cannot be simply rectified.

However, if you let yourself to be conscious, you may guarantee that all of your chakras are open at all times. Because you lack awareness, you are unable to comprehend the factors that contribute to the inactivity of your chakras. Take, for instance, the tale of a person who has just suffered the loss of a loved one. He ends up with bronchitis, and as a result of his coughing, he has discomfort in his chest every time he coughs. However, in the event that the individual is unable to make the connection between the death of a loved one due to bronchitis and his inability to open his chakras, they will remain closed. If he does, then he will acknowledge and respect the mourning process, and he will treat it alongside the physical problem that he is currently dealing with. As a result, he will recover much more quickly. Therefore, being aware of the chakras is a necessary step toward activating a chakra that is now dormant.

Methods Of Breathing That Will Assist You In Keeping Your Chakras Open

The most efficient methods, such as breathing into the belly, require you to engage your abdominal muscles in order to transmit more energy and awareness. If you are able to learn and perfect this method, it will be beneficial to your overall wellbeing and health.

You will also discover that it is not simply the act of breathing itself that is significant, but also the ability to recall how to breathe well. The intention to maximize the advantages that come with the correct use of breathing methods should be the primary point of emphasis here. During the practice, it is essential to bring your awareness to the breath, since this is the single most critical factor in determining how well your mind, physical body, and soul are all able to function.

It is a beneficial practice that will assist you to enhance your health, boost your vitality, and bring greater awareness to your body. Belly breathing allows you to do all of these things.

What exactly does the belly breathing technique entail?

Put the tips of your index fingers and thumbs together, then position them just below your navel or in the region of your second chakra that is right above the area of your pubic region. Imagine that you are breathing in and out while touching this place. When you breathe into your belly, you'll experience a richer and more profound sense of breath. In addition to that, it will assist you in providing your breath with the ideal direction. When you are laying down or standing up, it is much simpler to breathe into your stomach than of your chest. You may also practice while seated, however it is more difficult since you can end up filling your chest rather than your belly.

Pay attention to how you are breathing to ensure that you are inflating your stomach rather than your chest.

It is a frequent and natural mental image to see one's breath travelling from the lower abdomen to the upper chest, then to the crown, and finally out of the tops of our heads. It is for this reason why, when we breathe deeply, we elevate our chests to allow more air into our lungs so that they may become fully saturated. We often learn to soothe our nervous systems and significantly cut down on tension and worry.

When you breathe in through your nose and out through your mouth, however, you release all of your positive energy, also known as prana, into the surrounding air. If you breathe out, you won't be able to reap the benefits of strengthening your chakras. You may opt to breathe out if you feel that your chakras are already powerful and well balanced. If this is the case, it's perfectly OK.

NOTE: To practice belly breathing, picture exhaling through your mouth and then do the opposite. Instead of taking a big breath in and then releasing it, try drawing your breath inwards and downwards, then drawing it all the way into your stomach.

In some situations, there are those who breathe deeply from the chest, while others breathe from the abdomen. If you consider yourself to be someone who breathes deeply from the chest, you should aim to minimize the amount that you elevate your chest when you breathe. As you let your breath out, your tummy should fall in. At first, it may not be easy, but putting in more practice will help you become more proficient with the method. It is also OK for you to elevate your chest, but you need to make sure that your abdominal muscles are working quickly.

Some individuals have a propensity to clutch their bellies, particularly when they are motivated by the desire to seem to be thinner than they really are. They are unaware that they are harboring powerful emotions in the region of their belly, which leads to issues with the second chakra later on. The harboring of sentiments that are not acceptable is situated deep inside the center of our selves. These suppressed and unrecognized feelings will eventually manifest themselves in our bodies as illnesses if they are not dealt with.

People who have been through traumatic experiences may find it challenging, frightening, or unpleasant to practice belly breathing. It is crucial for individuals who are having trouble to get competent therapy if they feel they need it.

A Sacral Chakra That Is Both Open And Balanced

An person who has an open sacral chakra will feel feelings, as well as have a healthy body and mind. These benefits may be attained by engaging in activities that activate the Svadhistana. Due to the fact that the individual has coped with the process of self-realization, the individual will also experience profound sentiments of joy, creativity, optimism, sexuality, and sensuality. They are unafraid to embrace themselves and have a firm grasp on their own personality, capabilities, and boundaries. This individual is able to meet their own emotional needs without the assistance of others and feels comfortable interacting with others in a variety of contexts. When your sacral chakra is in harmony, you are able to place your faith in the people around you and communicate your most private emotions. Appreciate the fact that you are able to contribute freely without anticipating receiving anything in return. The capacity to comprehend what it is that sets off our feelings and to have some degree of control over those feelings is necessary for achieving a balanced state in the sacral chakra. I can have deep and meaningful relationships. I must nurture both my body and mind. I deserve to be admired, loved, and treated kindly. These are some examples of affirmations that can inspire emotional behavior and creativity. I have control over my emotions. I cannot control the behavior of others, but I can control how I react to it. I must nurture my own creativity. I can experience pleasure by simply being myself.

A Sacral Chakra that is Working Overtime

People that are too emotional, hedonistic, and manipulative have a sacral chakra that is operating at an excessively high level. They desire to generate their own sources of pleasure, even if it is not an appropriate moment to experience any kind of pleasure at all. Their needs take precedence above any form of logic or respect for the welfare of other people. This is especially detrimental given that their needs are influencing their actions, which in turn has a negative impact on the individuals in their immediate environment.

A Sacral Chakra That Is Blocked

A person who is suffering a blocked chakra will always feel alone and lonely, and they will have a severe phobia of getting close to other people. Feelings of inadequacy and uncertainty might be brought on by having a limited sexual life and a lack of creative expression.

This individual will struggle to express themselves in any form since they will keep their inhibitions to themselves and will find it difficult to do so. As time passes and the person's sacral chakra falls more out of harmony, they will acquire inclinations to be reliant on the emotional support of others, and these tendencies will become more pronounced with time. Due to the fact that the Svadhisthana chakra is in charge of the reproductive organs, adrenal glands, and the majority of the organs located in the pelvic region, any disorders that affect any of these organs lead to a sacral chakra that is out of alignment.

The fact that it is connected to one's emotions as well as their creative potential is an intriguing aspect of this chakra. It may be found in the pelvic region, close to the area that houses the genitalia. In life, your mental state is often tied to your feelings as well as your creative output. Because of this, many people believe that the mind, and not the body, is where emotions first begin. It is possible for this chakra to get blocked, which may lead to very outgoing behavior, such as promiscuity and living a wild lifestyle. It also relates to feelings of inadequacy and a lack of self-love, both of which may cause a person to be unable to establish close and meaningful relationships with other people as well as trust in the intentions of other people.

The top, or crown, chakra

The crown chakra is the most important one for us to focus on right now since it is situated directly above your head. You will need some time to get used to it, but you may experience it right now if you want to. For almost a half minute, rest your hand on top of your head, just above where your hair would reach. You should feel a warmth on your palm that is comparable to the warmth that comes from a candle flame. This warmth should not be felt whether you rest your hand straight on your head or if you hold your palm slightly higher. The hue of your Crown chakra may be anything from violet to white to gold, depending on your own preferences. It makes no difference whether you are unsure in the beginning. As you continue to work with your chakras, you will become more familiar with the hue associated with your Crown chakra.

Your link to the Divine, your higher intellect, and the key to a deeper awareness of who you are may all be found in the Crown chakra, which is referred to as Sahasrara in Sanskrit.

The origin and development of Chakras

If we want to know when chakras were initially acknowledged as a component of a person's ethereal and energetic body, we are going to have to go a very long way back in time. And after that, we wouldn't have a clue about anything since nobody is aware of this truth. What we do know is that an ancient Hindu document has the first known reference of chakras in the modern sense in which we define the term. That does not make the chakra system anything that is exclusive to Hinduism. Other societies, ranging from Japan and Korea in the east to Africa and Native American culture in the west, all have very similar notions and practices that mirror the chakra system we'll utilize today. These other civilizations may be found all over the world.

The religion of Hinduism

The Vedas, which are a collection of ancient Hindu literature, provide the first known written account of chakras. This description introduces the idea that chakras are energy vortices and powerhouses that are located inside each of us. In this section, you will also find references to shakti, which is also known as the kundalini energy. At a certain point in your journey toward spiritual enlightenment, the kundalini energy will emerge from your root chakra and go through the rest of your chakras, awakening any chakras that may have been inactive before.

The Upanishads, which were written more than 3,000 years ago, make reference to the subsequent development of the Hindu chakra system. This would be the point at which one would introduce nadis, which are lines that carry energy and connect the chakras. It wasn't until centuries later that these lines were given their energy carrying and psychological powers in Buddhist teachings; the ancient literature simply refers to them as "breath channels."

As we go through the ages during which India saw significant transformations, several schools of thought evolved, each with a unique perspective about the number of chakras that humans possess and the duties that are performed by those chakras. Ideas traveled, were shared, and had an impact on faiths and beliefs practiced not just locally but even internationally.

The Buddhist religion

Let's fast forward to the time of Medieval Buddhism, which discussed just four chakras and considered the activation of the kundalini to be a crucial milestone in the development of spirituality and psychic ability. Padmas were the names given to each of the chakras in this text. This approach provided us with the mental picture of the chakra in the form of a lotus, which we use for our meditations.

Tibetan Buddhism went in a somewhat different direction, popularizing Tantric ways of obtaining mastery over chakras, the flow of pranic life energy, and the activation of the kundalini, in order to accomplish the goal of experiencing joy via the activation of links between the mind, body, and spirit. These techniques also placed an emphasis on the spiritual and emotional development that might result from dealing with chakras. This school's goal was to achieve complete mental, physical, and spiritual freedom by using methods like as meditation, mandalas, mantras, symbols, and stages with a predetermined order.

The Chakra at the Crown

The seventh chakra center, similar to the sixth chakra center, links us to higher or alternative planes of existence; but, the connection established by the seventh chakra center is of a more varied and comprehensive kind. For the purpose of reaching complete enlightenment, the Crown chakra establishes a direct connection with either Source or our own Higher Selves. One way to think of the Higher Self is as an other version of oneself that understands everything about them, from the innermost parts of their existence to the things they present to the outside world. It comprehends you on a deeper level than you do yourself, and it really hopes that you find fulfillment in life and continue to grow as a person. You and your Higher Self are one and the same person; the only difference between the two is that you have your awareness anchored in the physical world, whilst your Higher Self exists on a far higher level of existence, thus the term. This is why you are experiencing this phenomenon. Not only does this provide absolute insight, but it also grants you vast knowledge to apply that clarity effectively. The location of the Crown chakra is often shown as being at the very top of the head or floating slightly above it. Despite its name, the Crown chakra is associated with thought rather than any particular element. Its component is the act of thinking itself. Consider the implications of that for a while, all right?

With its emphasis on being One with all that has been created, the Saharara places a primary focus on universal connectivity as its primary concept. When one comes to this awareness, they are able to achieve inner peace and a general reduction in fear. It is essential to keep in mind that the knowledge gained here is not on an intellectual level, but rather a more general comprehension of the functions that are played by every living creature in the universe. The Crown chakra is the location where the exchange of cosmic energy and the life energy of an individual takes place, which strengthens one's connectedness to everyone. The Saharara, which acts as a natural type of receptor for energies that are freely flowing throughout the cosmos, takes in this energy and turns it into power, which enables us to transcend our physical boundaries. When we have reached the transcendent level, our awareness "pushes out" into the vastness of the cosmos, giving forth life energy to be accepted by everyone. This happens when we have become one with the universe. It is a cycle of flowing energy that maintains life, both physical and spiritual, across the whole of the known cosmos. This cycle can be found in every part of the universe.

The inability to maintain a healthy balance in the Third Eye chakra may result in a disconnection from the physical world and a preference for living purely in the mind. You start to feel an almost total disconnection from the material world, even your own body. It goes without saying that this has the potential to severely damage any relationships with other people. You could even find that you are unable to stick to any kind of objective or continuous plan of action at all throughout this time. It is possible to get severed from one's spiritual connection, leaving one firmly entrenched in the physical element. Headaches, migraines, nerve pain, sleeplessness, depression, and even potential schizophrenia are some of the physical symptoms that express themselves more often than others.

One would do well to meditate on a regular basis in order to ward against certain sorts of illness. Also, give some thought to the idea of a glorious white light penetrating the crown of your head and becoming a part of it. Regularly engaging in any of these activities will activate your Brow chakra, so enabling it to function in an optimal manner. As is usually the case, practicing a wide range of yoga positions may help enhance the overall health of your chakras, in addition to maintaining the strength of your body. The presence of the aromas of sandalwood or myrrh in a space that you want to reside in can assist in the removal of any leftover obstructions. One more piece of advice: since the sun's light is such a potent source of natural energy, spending some time letting your Saharara soak up some of its rays can help boost its health.

The Seven Chakras

As was said previously, your body is comprised of seven primary chakras, all of which are arranged in line with your spine. You should take notice that in addition to these major energy sources, there are also additional lesser energy sites. The energy moves from the crown of your head all the way down to the base of your spine thanks to the chakras. If the body is not in a state of balance, the impacts of each of these chakras, which are each symbolized by a different hue, will become apparent.

A chakra is tied to each of the colors in that each vibrates to a specific frequency and reacts to various wavelengths of light (color). This is how a chakra is connected to the colors. As a result, some information about one's physical, emotional, mental, or spiritual state is included within each hue. This information is used in the process of chakra healing and balancing, which is accomplished via the use of color healing.

The seven chakras are described as follows below:

1. The sahasrara, often known as the crown chakra

The color violet is said to be representative of this chakra. You may locate it at the very top of your head. There is a connection between it and the cerebral cortex, as well as the central nervous system and the pituitary gland. This chakra is associated with knowledge, joy, and the concepts of understanding and acceptance. The link between you and God is also supposed to be established via this chakra. Additionally, it determines both one's own fate and the heavenly purpose for their lives. A blockage of this chakra may lead to a number of imbalances, including photosensitivity, migraines, neuralgia, epilepsy, mental disease, skin rashes, and difficulties with right-brain coordination and abnormalities, as well as other psychological issues. This chakra may be activated through journaling one's ideas, innovations, and visions, as well as by concentrating intently on one's dreams.

2. The brow chakra, often known as the third eye.

The color indigo, which is created by combining blue and red, is said to be representative of this chakra. It will sit in the middle of your forehead, somewhat higher than or at the same height as your eyes. The third eye chakra is associated with psychic abilities and intuition. It opens the mind to new ideas, questions, and knowledge. This chakra stores your dreams for this life as well as those from previous lives. If this chakra is blocked, it may result in difficulties with learning, sleep issues, sadness, a lack of foresight, and problems with one's ability to coordinate their movements. Stargazing and the observation of other indigo-colored items are two activities that might activate this chakra.

3. The visuddha, or throat, chakra

The area of your neck houses the fifth chakra, known as the throat chakra. This chakra is associated with the color turquoise or blue. This chakra is related to your neck, arms, shoulders, thyroid, hands, and parathyroid glands, and it is involved with communication, self-expression, creativity, and judgment. This chakra is responsible for both external and internal listening, as well as change, cleansing, and the synthesis of ideas. It is possible for this chakra to get blocked, which may result in swollen glands, thyroid imbalances, hyperactivity, influenza and fevers, infections, and hormonal abnormalities such as mood swings. The throat chakra may be activated by engaging in activities such as singing, poetry, painting, and stamp collecting; having meaningful discussions; and making use of objects that are blue.

4. The anahata, or heart, chakra Thecolor green is associated with the anahata, or heart, chakra. It is rather evident that it is situated inside your heart. This chakra is where compassion, love, peace, and harmony are found at their core. The majority of Asians believe that it is where the soul resides. The thymus gland, the heart, the lungs, the arms, and the hands are all connected to the heart chakra. When we feel love for someone, it is because of our heart chakra. Blocking this chakra may lead to

problems with breathing and the heart, as well as breast and heart cancer, high blood pressure, chest discomfort, and even inhumanity, unprincipled conduct, or a lack of compassion. To clear this chakra's blockage, try going on walks in natural settings, spending time with your loved ones, and making use of things that are green or feature the color green, such as donning green clothes.

5. The chakra known as the solar plexus (manipura).

You may locate this chakra only a few inches above your navel, in the region of your solar plexus, and it has a golden tint. Your muscles, pancreas, adrenal glands, and digestive system are all involved in this condition. This chakra is where all of your feelings and emotions are stored and processed. This energy area is connected to the emotions of pleasure, laughter, power, and rage that you experience. Your capacity to succeed, your sensitivity, and your drive are all contained in this region. If this chakra is blocked, you may encounter difficulties with your memory, digestive issues, ulcers, hypoglycemia, constipation, anxiousness, diabetes, rage, and frustration. These symptoms might be caused by a lack of circulation of energy.

Reading instructive books, enrolling in courses, engaging in mental puzzles, getting enough of sunlight, and taking part in detoxification programs are all excellent ways to keep the energy flowing effectively through this chakra. Utilizing things that are yellow in hue, such as wearing clothing that is yellow, is another way to assist in maintaining the flow of energy.

This chakra is represented as an orange hue and is located between your navel and your spine. It is also known as the sacral chakra, the navel chakra, and the spleen chakra. The kidneys, the lower abdomen, the bladder, the reproductive organs, the glands, and the circulatory system are all connected to this condition. It is involved with your feelings and emotions, which are represented by pleasure, desire, sexuality, creativity, and procreation. These are all important aspects of your life. An insufficient flow of energy to this chakra may lead to concerns such as alcohol and drug misuse, eating disorders, depression, lower back pain, Candida and yeast infections, asthma and allergic reactions, urinary problems, frigidity, impotence, and sensuality issues. This may also show itself as sexual guilt, compulsive behavior, and several other emotional issues.

You may improve the flow of energy to this chakra by taking warm baths with essential oils, getting a massage, engaging in water aerobics, and making use of orange objects and practices, such as donning orange clothing.

7. The Muladhara Chakra, also known as the Root Chakra.

Your coccyx is the location of the root chakra, which is a fiery-red energy center at the very base of your spine. It is connected to your life and addresses issues with the physical and material world, as well as concerns of security and your capacity to advocate for yourself. An imbalance in this chakra may result in symptoms such as lethargy, anemia, sadness, soreness in the lower back, numbness in the feet and hands, and recurrent bouts of the common cold.

This chakra may be activated by getting enough rest, engaging in physical activity, creating art, or working in the garden. As is often the case, donning items of clothes that are red may also be of assistance in enhancing the energy flow inside your root chakra.

Third Method: Praying

In case you were under the impression, you say prayers each and every day. Whether you believe in gods or not, regardless of who you are. It's possible that you'll ask, but how? Even if you are an atheist, you still believe in something. This something could be money or physics or even history or math, and unconsciously, you start making this thing so big that it's your god now, and your daily thoughts toward this thing are prayer. This is because the human is programmed to believe in something. Simply relying on something for direction and believing that this thing will be the reason behind your happiness, success, and being in peace, and thinking that because of this, your daily thoughts are revolved around this thing, a significant portion of your day, this alone is prayer, doesn't require you to get down on your knees or raise your hands in the air. This is prayer.

Some individuals are under the impression that all they need to do to be considered believers is to read their Bible or Quran, attend religious services weekly, and pray five times a day at a mosque or church. If you want to know what you believe in at this now, all you have to do is observe your thoughts for a week and see what they are focused on. If you are able to put in more effort and write things down in order to be more persistent, that would be even better.

Let's move on to the power of prayer now that we've established what it is, what it does, and why what you believe in determines how you spend your time every day. Researches have provided a lot of proof that prayer is highly strong. Starting with Andrew Newberg's brain scan, which reveals the difference between a believer in god's brain and a person who does not believe in god's brain and how prayer transforms the brain, researchers have proved that prayer is quite effective. The scan had demonstrated that the nuns' and Buddhists' brains were more engaged during prayer, particularly in the lobes and to be more precise, the orientation region. However, the scan also showed that the nuns' brains were even more activated owing to the vocal prayer and mixing between imagining and reciting.

Pray, explain to God and the world what it is that you desire, and ask for clarity, purification, and to have your spirit and soul purified. Through prayer, you are able to become one with God, which in turn enables you to become one with divine love, divine light, and divine grace.

Your life will change for the better if you pray consistently for ten minutes a day, but there are some guidelines that must be followed in order for your prayers to be answered:

The reality is that God, the cosmos knows you so well that it even knows you better than you know yourself. When you pray, be honest, tell God what you truly want, and explain to him why you want it, as well as what will happen and improve as a result of its being manifested. However, when you clarify why you want the thing you are asking for and what will happen when you get it, you are only reminding yourself of these things and giving yourself more clarity; you are not helping God in any way by doing so. If you are honest, God will give you anything you ask for.

- Maintain Your Regularity: Magic takes place when there is inconsistency, and without it, nothing takes place. Is it possible to get a degree without physically attending classes or travelling to school on a regular basis? Is it possible to love another person even if you don't spend a lot of time with them? No, because there are rules and regulations in life that you need to follow in order to acquire what it is that you want.

Pray aloud: the sound of your own voice has a great deal of influence. Did you know that you have a unique voiceprint just like you have a fingerprint? When you recite a prayer and ask for what you desire using your voice, your brain becomes active, and magic occurs. If you didn't know it, you should.

The Third Chakra, Located In The Throat.

The color blue is said to symbolize the throat chakra, which is associated with speech as well as the expression of one's own personality. This chakra is in charge of regulating how intensely our facial expressions get while we are interacting with other people and communicating with them. If you are able to open this chakra, you will have an easier time communicating with other people. You may anticipate improving your ability to communicate in an unrestricted manner.

People that have a healthy and open throat chakra exude an air of self-assurance. This quality endows them with likability and magnetism, and it is often the quality that enables them to distinguish themselves from the other individuals in the group. People whose neck chakras are open often express themselves creatively and have an interest in the visual arts or performing arts.

If the energy in this chakra is not flowing as it should, you may experience shyness and find it difficult, if not impossible, to speak out in large groups of people. People who suffer from stage fright often have issues related to a restricted throat chakra.

Your self-confidence will most likely suffer as a result of this, and you will find it tough to acknowledge when you have been unsuccessful and much more challenging to "start over." It is common for people who are going through such terrible times to withdraw within themselves and become more self-absorbed. Isolation and the utter lack of a social life are the only possible outcomes that can come from doing something like that. In addition to this, having a blocked throat chakra may lead to vices such as compulsive lying.

People whose throat chakra is overactive tend to be chatty to the point that it makes others around them uncomfortable. Their inflated sense of self-esteem gives them the appearance of being exceedingly haughty and superior. People who have this trait tend to speak more and listen less. They lack depth of thought and are often looked down upon by others around them. An overactive throat chakra not only makes you a poor listener, but it also functions as a huge barrier to learning new things and venturing into uncharted territory.

Because of this, opening the throat chakra may help you achieve a required balance in your expressiveness and social behaviour. This simple practice can assist you in opening your throat chakra so that you can take advantage of all of the advantages that come with doing so.

Repeat the position you have been practicing throughout the workouts thus far, which is to sit on your knees. Allow your hands to hang at either side of your body in a relaxed and loose manner. Make an effort to get your body to loosen up and relax so you can feel better. Now, carefully lift your hands to shoulder height and interlace your fingers on the palms of both hands so that they form a cross. Be sure that your thumbs are pointing straight up and are touching one another. Once you have reached that posture, you should attempt to raise yourself up a little bit.

You should bring your hands up to your neck like this. Relax and make an effort to regain your calm by focusing on the throat chakra and all of the beneficial impacts it has on our body, in particular, as well as on life, in general. After you have achieved a state of relaxation, it is time to begin reciting the "HAM" mantra. When you are reciting the mantra, you should make sure that your mind is free of any thoughts about the outside world and that you are entirely concentrating on the function of the throat chakra.

If it is at all feasible, you should attempt to think on the positive impacts that this practice is having on your body while you are simultaneously releasing the negative effects of having a blocked throat chakra and having it opened. Maintain the same posture during the mantra practice, and do so until you can once again identify that sensation of cleanliness.

During this particular exercise, we strongly encourage our readers to maintain the steadiest possible control of both their hands and their heads. They will be better able to concentrate on the workout as well as the throat chakra itself as a result of this. The presence of your mind and your ability to exert control over your thoughts is the single most significant factor in determining the efficacy of your workouts, but even very straightforward advice like this may make a difference.

We hope that you are able to follow the recommendations and that you find it simple to incorporate them into your day-to-day activities. Let's move on to our last two chakras as fast as possible.

The Soul Star Chakra

The Fundamentals of the Soul Star Chakra

In the same vein as the Earth Star chakra, the Soul Star chakra is one of the energy centers that the vast majority of people are not particularly knowledgeable of. Both the Earth Star and the Soul Star chakras are termed "subpersonal" chakras since they are located outside of our physical bodies. The Soul Star chakra is quite similar to the Earth Star chakra.

The Soul Star chakra, often referred to as the Seat of the Soul, is the eighth chakra in human bodies and is located between six and twelve inches above the crown of the head. It is regarded as the portal via which we may access the upper worlds and the universe. You might think of this chakra as our link to our highest self, and it functions as a conduit between embodied experience and spiritual awareness. It is known as Vyapini in Sanskrit, which literally translates to "universal heart," and it is connected to the color magenta or dazzling white.

A Soul Star Chakra That Is in Good Health

When we have a Soul Star chakra that is in a state of balance, we are able to transcend the dualistic character of existence and become one with "all that is." Because we now have a better understanding of our soul purpose, we are able to lead lives that are more congruent with who we are at our core. Beliefs that constrained us in the past are no longer an issue, and we are free to go ahead with purpose.

Disharmonies in the Soul Star Chakra

If we have a blockage in the Soul Star chakra, we may have feelings of emptiness or a sensation that something is missing from our lives. It's possible that we become trapped and can't figure out what our mission in life is. An excessive amount of energy in the eighth chakra may manifest in ways that are similar to those of an overactive Crown chakra. These include an obsessive desire to be in a "enlightened" condition, detachment from the earth and physical reality, and a lack of direction. In a purely physical sense, we could suffer from headaches and dizziness on a regular basis.

Symptoms That Your Chakras Are Unbalanced As A Warnng To You

The seven energy centers, also known as chakras, are dispersed throughout the body. Since each of these chakras is placed in a different part of the body, each of these chakras is associated with a unique physiological condition and physical dysfunction. These energy centers contained not only our physical but also our mental and emotional fortitudes. Therefore, as soon as we start having certain bodily problems, it also begins to produce vulnerabilities in our emotional conduct. As soon as we expelled stale energy from the body, it was able to erase any feelings of stiffness or tightness that were experienced in the specific location of the body that was experiencing a malfunction.

When our energy centers are cleansed, our emotional state of mind may likewise become more in tune with reality. Maintaining harmony in the mind-body chakra is like to being on a roadway that goes in both directions. It is possible to encounter physical constraints or malfunctions in the body if you are hanging on to certain emotions, such as phobias, for an extended period of time.

Let's talk about opening up chakras that are blocked, also known as energy centers.

It is possible that certain energy points are blocked if you are experiencing some pain or stiffness in addition to persistent anxieties and feelings of anxiety associated to those fears.

To begin with the Root Chakra

A physical imbalance in this energy center may create difficulties in the leg, rectum, immune system, male reproductive organs, tailbone, and prostate glands. This is because it rests on the base of your spine and at your tailbone. People who have these imbalances are more prone to have problems with degenerative arthritis, sciatica, knee pain, constipation, and eating disorders. They may also have knee discomfort.

On the other hand, emotional imbalances include feelings that have an effect on fundamental survival demands such as the need for food, money, and shelter, with the capacity to provide for life's basics serving as the primary emphasis.

You will have a feeling of connection and safety to the material world when your root chakra is in a healthy state of balance.

The Sacral Chakra

The naval Chakra is the location of the Sacral Chakra, which is concerned with sexual energy as well as creative expression. It is also known as the chakra of partnership because it governs our interactions and connections with other people and maintains a balance in our capacity to both give and receive sensation and emotion. Around the age of seven, most children begin making interpersonal connections outside of the realm of their immediate families. This is the time when the Sacral Chakra begins to become active. These connections help us become more self-reliant and give us our first taste of the agency that comes with having choices. We begin to exercise control over our surroundings and acquire the ability to fend for ourselves as a result of the decisions that we make.

A healthy sacral chakra eliminates patterns of restricting negative behavior, which in turn leads to increased feelings of self-confidence and emotional stability and makes it possible for us to realize our full potential. In addition to putting us in touch with our inner selves or souls, it opens up the channels via which we may give and receive. It was never intended for us to spend our lives according to the dictates of our egos. Instead, our souls, also known as our authentic selves, are here to serve as a guidance for the ego. When our Sacral Chakra is healthy, balanced, and open, we no longer seek to the world outside of ourselves for direction and approval. In spite of the fact that we no longer care what other people think of us or our way of life, we find that we have grown friendlier, more cheerful, and have developed a real compassion for other people. We utilize our capacity for self-sufficiency to listen to the counsel our souls provide, cultivating healthy connections while placing ourselves on the route to pleasure and a sense of accomplishment as a result.

The Sacral Chakra, which is the energy center for imagination, creativity, and self-confidence, is a deciding element in the degree to which we are able to affect or are impacted by the outside world. Extreme sensitivity is a symptom of insufficient energy in the Sacral Chakra. We wallow in self-doubt, clinging to other people for support while developing characteristics of dread, shyness, timidity, mistrust, and helplessness. We have tremendous feelings of guilt over a range of topics, most notably sex, and as a result, we suppress our emotions and become resentful of people who are unable to see or respond to them. On the other hand, an excess of energy in the Sacral Chakra may result in a personality that is self-centered and self-indulgent. Aggression, an excessive fixation with sex, emotional explosiveness, and uncontrolled ambition are all signs of its presence. We start passing judgment on and criticizing other people, as well as becoming involved in the business of other people and seeking to control them.

The reproductive organs, the big intestines, the bladder, the pelvis and hips, the lower vertebrae, the mammary glands, and the lymphatic system are all associated with the Sacral Chakra. Also associated with this chakra is the lymphatic system. Infertility, back discomfort, breast cancer, and other disorders connected to these bodily parts are all examples of symptoms that may be attributed to an imbalance in the Sacral Chakra.

Now is the moment to change sentiments of unworthiness into self-confidence that may be productively used. It is necessary to heal the sacral chakra in order to improve both your romantic connections and your sexual life. This energy will free your imagination, allowing you to pursue whatever it is that drives you. It will release you from the shackles of the influences of the outer world and give you the opportunity to follow the lead of your most authentic and improved self.

Indicators And Problems Caused By An Unbalanced Root Chakra

Problems with your legs, foot, rectum, tailbone, or immune system might be symptoms of a physical imbalance in your Root Chakra. Problems with the prostate gland and other male reproductive systems are another possible symptom of this condition. Eating disorders, sciatica, constipation, knee pain, and degenerative arthritis are some symptoms that may develop as a consequence of an imbalance in the Root Chakra.

It's possible that you find yourself getting irritated easily, that your self-confidence is low, and that you're afraid of everything. It's possible that you don't have the desire to accomplish even the most basic of your objectives, and this might be a problem for you.

sentiments that are directly linked to your capacity to supply the bare essentials of existence for oneself, such as food, shelter, and money, may be brought on by emotional imbalances. These sentiments may make you question whether or not you will be able to survive.

How to Bring Your First Chakra Into Balance

You will experience feelings of being grounded and focused when your Root Chakra is in a state of balance. You will experience feelings of connection and support, as well as a sense of connectedness to your physical reality and a sense of safety and security within that world.

You will have a feeling of serenity and be prepared to deal with any challenges life throws at you when your Root Chakra is in a state of equilibrium. Your self-confidence will soar, and you will have an abundance of different types of energy.

Move it!

It makes no difference whether you can dance or if you can't dance. Simply put on some tunes and begin moving to the rhythm of the beat. Relax your thoughts, and give your body permission to accomplish what it has to do. It is possible that you may be amazed by how well your body is able to sync up with the song.

You will find that this is an effective method for bringing balance to your Root Chakra. If you feel the want to sing along, feel free to do so. The Throat Chakra is one of the chakras that may be purified via the use of singing.

It's Time for You to Look at the Big Picture

Make sure that you are imagining the color red, brightly shining at your Root Chakra, which is located at the base of your spine. Because the color red is at the core of the Root Chakra, you must ensure that you are visualizing the color red at your Root Chakra. This is the first step in cleansing and rebalancing your Root Chakra, which you can find more information about here.

You should begin with a fairly simple meditation that involves visualizing a strong, forceful, and brilliant red light at the base of your spine (tailbone). Imagine the light traveling down your legs until it reaches your feet, where it connects you firmly to the ground below.

Be sure to Keep it Tidy!

It is possible that you are unaware of how important taking a shower is in relation to the process of purifying your Root Chakra. Taking a shower or bath forces you to acknowledge and appreciate the physical you that you have.

Have a stroll on the meditative side.

- Get some exercise and go for a stroll. Make every effort to escape away from the sounds of civilized society. Find a trail, drive out into the countryside, or go to any other location where you may commune with the natural world. Relax and clear your mind while you stroll.

While you are progressing ahead in your walk, you should also be progressing forward mentally. Keep in mind that each time you take a step, your foot is lifting off the ground and making a new connection with the planet. This is a wonderful technique to clear your Root Chakra while also giving your mind a vacation from its usual activities.

Time for yoga

There are a number of different yoga positions that may be used in order to clear your root chakra. Since the tree stance is simple to achieve, we will focus on achieving that one in this lesson; however, you are welcome to try out other poses as well.

First, place the whole of your left foot onto your mat, and then, while maintaining a comfortable posture, raise your right foot up over your knee. At the same time, try to picture the color 'red.'

Make sure that your hip is pointing in a straight line front of you at all times, and then put your foot anywhere on your leg other than on your knee. Check that your toes are tucked in properly.

To really make the tree pose your own, you shouldn't be scared to be creative with it and make it your own. You may also try putting your right leg into a half lotus position as an alternative. First, ensure that your abdominal muscles are engaged, and then reach your arms over your head. Check that your elbows are in a straight line. Because of this, you will be able to rotate your hands, which will work your triceps muscles.

The most important thing for you to do is to have a sense of being linked to the ground. Keep your body in the tree stance for ten to fifteen breaths. Alter your position, then continue.

When And Where Exactly Did The Chakras First Appear?

The Hindu culture is where the concept of chakras first appeared, and these energy centers have profound ties to the practices and rites that are observed by Hindus. These customs and rites have been carried out consistently over the ages. Chakras have always left a significant imprint on yoga as a practice thanks to the many traditions around them.

When and where exactly did the information gather take place?

There are a great number of academics who have consistently been working toward the goal of accumulating more knowledge about the chakras. They have realized that the Upanishads are the source of each and every one of these pieces of knowledge. These have been compiled from the Hindu writings known as the Vedas, and they include the most vital precepts. These had been put together many years ago with the intention of disseminating information and wisdom. They are thereafter known as the Rig, Sama, Atharva, and Yajur Vedas respectively. It is sad that no one knows for certain when the Vedas were written down. The sole piece of information that has been found on the origin of the Upanishads is that they were composed around the seventh century. According to the historical record, there were 108 different Upanishads written. There are thirteen books in the Upanishad that deal with the Chakras and supply enormous amounts of information about them. These texts may be found in the same place as the Upanishad. It is only when you give the material contained in the

Upanishad your whole attention that you will be able to comprehend the chakras in a better way.

The Third Eye Chakra, also known as the Brow Chakra, may be found in the space between a person's eyes and in the middle of the forehead. There is no guarantee that there is a physical eye located anywhere on the forehead. The light chakra and the center of the mind are both known as ajna. It has some kind of relationship with the brain. It relates to the senses of sight and hearing and is concerned with insight, intellectualism, intuition, and the ability to visualize. Here is where we think, where we make choices, where we dream, and where we envisage.

You have achieved intellectual realization when your energy travels to the Ajna chakra. You have a good grasp of the situation. You have an accurate perception of how things are. Once you start to view things for what it really is, you will find that it brings you calm.

Because it enables you to see things as they really are, Ajna is often referred to as the "third eye."

The appearance of both eyes should not be trusted. They will make you perceive things in a manner that is essential for your continued existence. They will not let you see anything as it really is in its entirety. When your energy moves into the Third Eye Chakra, you have the ability to perceive things as they really are.

Indecisiveness, hasty judgments, leaping to conclusions, forgetfulness, a lack of common sense, and an inability to see the wider picture are some of the symptoms of a Brow Chakra that is not functioning properly.

A mind that is too active might block the flow of energy via the Third Eye Chakra. If you find yourself thinking things like "You shouldn't have done this or that" or

"I'm not good enough" or "This is not going to work at all" along with other unfavorable ideas, this is a sign that your ajna chakra isn't functioning properly. Put an end to that voice that is instructing you how to think.

Illusion also serves to stop an unhealthy state of Ajna. The idea that we are separate from one another is this world's most powerful delusion. Things that seem to be distinct from one another yet are, in reality, merged into a single entity. Every living thing is exactly the same. We are all linked together. We belong to the same human race. There is a thing among us that is referred to as a collective awareness.

The difficulty is that we continue to behave as though we are split apart. However, the reality is that everything is interconnected. Even the apparent distinction between the four components is an optical illusion. If you let your thoughts wander, you'll find that all the components are indistinguishable from one another. Free yourself from all of your own self-imposed delusions.

To cleanse this Chakra, you must first be receptive to receiving the guidance of the divine. Divine insight and direction are always accessible to us, but the majority of the time, we let other things or even ourselves to stand in the way of receiving them.

Imagine a blue hue while you are meditating and concentrating along the center of your forehead or on the third eye. Imagine it as a sphere of energy that exists inside you and gradually expands throughout your whole body. Allow it to go through your other chakras and out into the world until it touches your fingertips. Now repeat the sound "EI" again and over. You may open yourself up to the divine knowledge by saying affirmations such as "I am in touch with my inner guidance" or "I listen to my deepest wisdom" or "I am at peace."

Keeping your eyes open and focusing your attention on a distant or insignificant target, such as the flame of a candle, is one of the practices that may be done to cleanse the Chakra. Simply concentrate on the task at hand and let go of any and all other ideas that may enter your head. The term for this kind of activity is trataka. Lie on your back on the grass at night and look up at the sky for a different and enjoyable option. Be sure to fix your attention on only one star at a time.

The Manipura, or Solar Plexus, is the subject of Chapter 3.

The Practice of Conscious Breathing

Find a sitting posture that is comfortable for you, especially one in which your legs are crossed and you are seated on the floor. Pay attention to how you are breathing. Take note of the movement in your stomach as well as your chest as you breathe in and out. Maintain your normal breathing while placing one hand on your tummy and the other hand on your chest. While you are doing this:

1.) Picture what's going on within your body when you take a breath in and then let it out.

2.) Permit yourself to think that you have control over your breathing and, as a result, the expansion and contraction of your stomach and chest. Consider how you're feeling now that you have more control over your breathing.

The Chakra of Self-Control

The ManiPura, or Solar Plexus, is the third energy node in our body and is positioned only a few inches above the navel. It is also more popularly known as the Sacral Plexus. This Chakra is related to our emotional lives, but it also controls how we see ourselves, which is possibly a more significant function. It controls our levels of self-esteem and self-confidence, as well as how we understand our own sense of value. Therefore, as you should hopefully be starting to understand, the Solar Plexus deals primarily and in part with our sense of vision, as well as our personal strength and our ability to exert control.

A significant number of persons who have adopted the concept of chakras believe that successful people—those who thrive in their occupations, have discovered pleasure via their own means, or are financially independent—have a particularly active Solar Plexus. It is undeniably a thought-provoking proposition. After fact, the majority of successful people do have high self-esteems, approach challenging circumstances with confidence, and have a strong sense of their own sense of worth.

Activate Your Solar Plexus Chakra

When the energy in our Solar Plexus is under check, we are able to flourish. We face difficult circumstances with a special clarity, we solve problems in an effective manner, and we have faith in our own ability to choose the appropriate strategy. Confidence and a sense of self-worth, on the other hand, might briefly vanish along with the Solar Plexus when it becomes imbalanced.

Signs and Symptoms of a Solar Plexus Chakra That Is Closed

Disorganized thinking

Depressive state

Dominance is the outcome of having a Solar Plexus that is overactive.

The dread of being rejected

Lack of capacity to make choices or judgments.

a deficit in one or more of the following: self-esteem; self-confidence; and/or self-worth

Passivity is the outcome of a Solar Plexus that is not functioning properly.

Foods That Help Open the Solar Plexus

foods that are yellow in hue, such as maize and cornmeal

Oatmeal and granola are examples of grains.

Whole grain bread and raisins are both good sources of fiber.

Tea made with chamomile

Exercises That Help Open the Solar Plexus

Stepping out: Dancing needs a certain amount of self-control since we need to regulate how our feet move to the rhythm of the music, how our legs carry us across the dance floor, and how our arms move so that they are not just hanging limp at our sides. Dancing demands exactly the perfect amount of physical control to throw open our Solar Plexus or bring it back to the state of equilibrium it was in when we were first born. It doesn't really matter what kind of dance you perform; as long as you're moving and maintaining control of your body, dancing is a practice that tends to be quite beneficial.

The "Boat Pose" is another exercise that requires us to have total control of our bodies and is an excellent remedy for anybody who may have an imbalance in their Solar Plexus. The following is something that you will wish to do:

1. Before beginning this exercise, choose an area on the floor that is level, firm, and supporting all at the same time.

2. While keeping your bottom firmly planted on the floor, progressively rise the upper and lower parts of your body until they create the shape of a V. 3. Hold this position for as long as you feel comfortable.

3. Extend both of your arms so that they are perpendicular to the ground in front of you. Allow the inside of each outstretched arm to softly touch the outside of each thigh. Do not support your body or your legs by using your arms to hold them up.

4. Maintain this posture for the next thirty seconds. Focus your attention on the way you are breathing.

5. After the first thirty seconds, drop both your upper and lower halves back to the floor in a gradual and controlled manner. After you have rested for one minute, repeat the exercise another two more times, bringing the total number of repetitions to three.

When I initially started practicing meditation on the chakras, I began by focusing on my third eye. When I was a young adolescent, I struggled with debilitating headaches in addition to severe depression. At this point in my life, I was struggling with pretty much every aspect of it, and I really wanted some respite. At the time, while I was already doing Kundalini yoga, I did not have a complete understanding of my chakras. My yoga instructor suggested that I attempt to open my third eye chakra so that I might get some relief from my headaches and from the despair I've been experiencing.

Unless a person has a significant ailment similar to the ones I was suffering, I would not generally suggest that they begin with this chakra. However, in my case, it was necessary. Due to the fact that I am an Indigo, this was essential to my continued existence. My symptoms improved rapidly, and I noticed that I was beginning to have more Third Eye openings. On the other hand, if all of your succeeding chakras are closed, you won't be able to open your Third Eye chakra completely even if you try. Seeing auras was the first indication that I had successfully opened my Third Eye when I was younger. When I observed that my progress had leveled out, I felt it was time to start working on my first chakras so that I could return to my Third Eye chakra with a fresh perspective on who I am. This has been an absolutely incredible adventure.

The Third Eye is the portal through which we communicate with our higher selves. You should first educate yourself about the chakra system before beginning the process of accessing the Third Eye. This will enable you to have a complete understanding of what to anticipate after it has been unlocked, as well as what you need to be wary of. When you are a teenager, you will first have the opportunity to open the chakras associated with your Third Eye. The Third Eye was often referred to as the "seed of the soul" by ancient people. We now know that it has a direct connection to the pineal gland, which is responsible for regulating your circadian cycles as well as the quantities of melatonin and serotonin in your body.

The unlocking of the Third Eye is not something that can be done by just anybody. If you are content with the way things are in your life right now and have no desire for change, you should not think about opening your third eye.

We are only able to see less than one percent of the electromagnetic spectrum, and we are only able to hear less than one percent of the acoustic spectrum. After you've opened your Third Eye, your experience of the world around you will no longer be the same. Unlocking your Third Eye could be the right choice for you if you wish to communicate with the other 99% of the population. Please do not open your Third Eye if you have no intention of quitting your 9-to-5 job. As soon as you begin to open your Third Eye, you will become aware that life consists of much more than your typical 9-to-5 routine and that there are many options available to you. Please do not open your Third Eye if you have a strong need for processed junk food. When you have completed the process of opening your Third Eye, you will be able to see the truth in everything that you put into your body. When you open what is known as your "Third Eye," you will begin to realize how everything is related to one another. Do not even bother trying to open your Third Eye if you have no intention of giving up your normal television shows and books. The process of unlocking your Third Eye will need you to think more critically about everything you take in, including the information.

When someone initially activates their pineal gland, which is the process of unlocking their Third Eye chakra, many individuals report hearing a loud popping sound in the centre of their brain. This is also known as the "aha" moment. There is a connection between the pineal gland and the Third Eye chakra. It is also extremely usual to have a severe pressure as well as tingling in the centre of your forehead after unlocking, and this sensation may continue for many days. This is an indication that you are beginning to open your Third Eye. You need to get yourself ready for it. Visions of objects that may be regarded as being beyond of our planet are the most unsettling sign. If you are not aware of this impact, it has the potential to be scary. This resulted in clairvoyance as well as glimpses of ghosts and other spirits. There have been reports of people who claim to have seen beings from other dimensions. Unlocking your Third Eye is another way to develop your psychic powers. Psychic abilities may also be inherited. Astral projection and the perception of auras are potentially potential symptoms of this condition. When you open your Third Eye, you will notice an immediate increase in your level of awareness.

When one meditates, lights and visuals may also come into their field of vision.

Any images that you could encounter might easily become overpowering. After being unlocked, it could be tough to get a handle on it at first. Before you can unleash the power of your Third Eye chakra, you need to ensure that you are well prepared. During this procedure, if you are not cautious, you may lock your root chakra, which is a possibility given that your root chakra is locked by fear. Please be as patient as possible while this door is being unlocked.

You have to give your Third Eye chakra a lot of attention if you want it to become activated.

Positions of Meditation

Assume a laying posture on a yoga mat and go into SalambaSarvangasana, also known as the supported shoulder stand. You may give your shoulders some support by utilizing a folded piece of fabric. In the meanwhile, make sure that your head is touching the ground.

You should start by bending your knees, and then you should swing your hips upward. Put your legs so that they are hanging above.

Put your hands behind your center back to give yourself some support.

Raise one of your legs and repeat on the other. Check that your feet are positioned such that your toes are facing upward.

After that, elevate your other leg while continuing to keep the support on your middle back.

Pay close attention to the manner that you breathe while you are doing this. Put your focus on your chest, and as it moves up and down, watch your eyes move with it.

Imagine that there is a flame of a bluish-white hue blazing in the very center of your chest. Repeat the word "Ham" again and over.

Hold this posture for as long as possible, up to two minutes.

After then, you are at liberty to lower each of your legs in turn.

Every time you put yourself in this situation, you are having an effect on the part of your life that is in charge of determining your own particular truths.

Having No Holdings Back

Although the concept of letting go is familiar to all of us, the actual act of doing so may be challenging. When it comes to this topic, we are all hypocrites because we all advise one other to let things go, but at the same time, we all cling to things that would be better off being left in the past. She tells me one thing, then when I repeat it back the way I heard and comprehended what she said, she promptly informs me that she did not say that. My supervisor is a bundle of inconsistencies. I take great satisfaction in the fact that I am an excellent listener. The majority of the individuals in my life have remarked that I am an excellent listener. Almost all of it is, with the exception of my supervisor Judy. This, in turn, is a major source of irritation for the two of us since we are forever getting our thoughts and actions confused with one another. The majority of the issue stems from her perception that I speak too much, whilst I get the impression that she speaks too little.

I have no problems getting ready for work each morning, and everything goes swimmingly most of the day... until she shows there. The moment she does that, my muscles immediately tighten up since she consistently takes the wrong meaning from what I say. Judy is under the impression that I consistently misunderstand what she is saying to me. It's very funny when you think about it. I never know whether to laugh or weep, and it's exhausting trying to decide which one to do! Because this battle is a daily reality, it is tough because of it. However, until I feel like searching for another employment, I'm stuck with her, and she's stuck with me. Neither of us has a choice in the matter. Do you get a sense of how excited we are about that? No? Then it's time to resign. That sums it up well. How am I supposed to put into practice what I'm teaching here and urge you to let go of your everyday frustrations when I face my own each week, Monday through Friday?

It is true that I was not dealing with it very well. We do not communicate in the same language, Judy and I. To tell you the truth, we do. It's merely a matter of speaking various accents. There are a great number of variations on the Spanish language within the Latin culture. Castilian, Andalusian, and Murcian are the three varieties of Spanish that are commonly used in Spain. There are an even greater number in the more compact locations. In the meanwhile, the Spanish that is used in the Caribbean is an altogether distinct variety of the language. Pronunciation is highly different, and they do not use the same vocabulary across the language. They could have had a common ancestor, but the passage of time, distance, and natural selection have resulted in irreconcilable differences between them.

So how did I succeed in letting go? I definitely began paying more attention to what was being said. There are occasions when we jump to the conclusion that we understand something when in reality we have just assumed certain things. I had to politely request that she calm down while she was explaining everything. Her instructions are sometimes given in a hurried manner, and once she finishes giving them, she rushes off to put out another fire. As a result, I frequently end up doing the incorrect thing because I try to fill in the gaps myself.

What I am concentrating on at the moment is, in all honesty, what it is that she wants from me. Judy would like it if I would speak less. In her world, having less possessions is preferable, and I'm simply trying to survive in it. I am also not going to give in to letting her make me anxious any longer. I tell her to pause and think before continuing if she takes anything she overheard me say to a client the wrong way. It's not easy when she has her own interpretation of what you just said, but my confidence comes from the knowledge that I'm excellent at what I do, and all she has to do is trust me.

The art of letting go is a lucrative industry. Songs have been written about it, whole sessions of therapy have been dedicated to it, and there are a million books on self-help on the subject. There is undeniable evidence that this is difficult for us to achieve. It is now the year 2018, yet we still do not have the technology to go through time and change the things that we did in the past that we regret. Do you really want to do that? Do you wish to make fundamental changes to the person you are right now? Whatever it is that happened that you wish you could alter, didn't other positive things follow it, which you valued much more as a result? Everyone needs to gain wisdom from their experiences. It is not intended for us to make any changes. Only be taught. Experience. Get over it.

All of these negative feelings—fears, wrath, humiliation, and embarrassment—stand between you and the benefits that are waiting for you. You will never progress or be able to go on to greater things in life as long as you continue to live with and indulge in your ego. This will prevent you from moving on. Don't you sometimes forget how closely your heart and your soul are connected? This negativity builds up on your physical body, mental well-being, and spiritual being like a thick coating of grime. As a result, the act of letting go of this negativity is something that requires effort, with each instance requiring a deliberate decision to do so.

You may accomplish this goal in a number of ways, one of which is to carry out the grounding practice that we attempted in the first chapter. You will improve in so many different ways if you give meditation a go; there is no reason not to.

The use of visualization is yet another powerful technique. If you imagine what you want to do before you start, it will assist your mind finish the stages.

The Hot Air Balloon

In the beginning of summer, there is a lovely warm day. You are now situated on the edge of a riverbank. While you are seated at the foot of a tree, the water gently trickles by, passing through the canal, over the rocks, and past you. The rough bark is rubbing up on your t-shirt, and you can feel it.

You are holding a balloon in your hand on which is written in marker everything you have said that you want to let go of. Relationships that have caused you pain, setbacks in your life, and anything else that comes to mind that you should write down. You go over the list, checking to see that everything is there. If it isn't, it doesn't matter; you may come back here whenever you feel the need to release anything from your life.

You take a deep breath in and slowly allow the string climb up through your fingers as you inhale.

Now exhale, and as you do, let the balloon to float away from you, bringing with it everything unpleasant and destructive that you have been hanging onto. Not any more. In an instant, you've made room in your life for the positive things to return by letting go of the negative things. More of it is definitely something we could use.

You may give the following a shot at any point. Writing anything down, no matter what it is, may be therapeutic. Putting words to paper can assist you in working through whatever it is that you are going through in a truly good manner. It is possible to become stuck in a train of thought that moves slowly and steadily in the wrong direction at times. Do you remember the mental haze? When I write anything down, I usually find that it teaches me things that I couldn't have known before. Dialoguing about a predicament may undoubtedly be of assistance. Writing, on the other hand, forces you to absorb the words in a new way because when you see them in front of you, when they are rendered in black and white, you can no longer deny the reality of the situation.

The Guide to Chakras

The following is an explanation of all of the primary chakras of the body, along with the characteristics that are often connected with each one. You may also utilize this list to assist you in diagnosing any specific issues that you may be having with a certain chakra imbalance that you may be experiencing.

1. The first chakra, or the root.

The chakra is situated underneath the body and the spine, namely in the region around the tailbone and the base of the spine. Symbolizes both our sense of being grounded and our basis in this world.concerns with safety, fundamental requirements for existence, and the ability to continue existing.

2. The Sacral Chakra is situated in the region of the lower belly, about two to three inches below the navel. Symbolizes

our connection to other people as well as our openness to trying new things, taking joy in things, and experiencing a sense of fulfillment.

3. The Solar Plexus Chakra is situated in the middle of the belly, directly below the rib cage. Symbolizes the sense of affluence and self-assurance that we have.

4. The Heart Chakra The heart chakra is located in the middle of our chest, just over our heart, and it is the hub of our emotions related to love, joy, and serenity.

5. Throat Chakra The Throat Chakra is located in the middle of the throat and is symbolic of our capacity to communicate with others, our self-expression, our confidence, and our understanding of the truth.

6. The Third Eye Chakra The third eye chakra is situated in the middle of the forehead, between the eyes. It is symbolic of our intuition, imagination, knowledge, and capacity to think and make judgments.

7. The third eye chakra

The crown chakra is the most powerful chakra in the body, and its location is at the topmost pinnacle of the head, just above the vertical line of the spine. It is a representation of our connection to the spiritual realm, as well as knowledge and happiness.

Contribute to the Regeneration of the Chakras of Others!

Not only can you use color therapy to rebalance and strengthen your own chakras, but you can also use it to assist improve the chakras of your family members, loved ones, and friends. When you see a member of your immediate or extended family going through a challenging period in their life, you may lend them a hand by making use of this resource. This kind of healing is known as "Distant Healing."

Exercise in Long-Distance Healing:

When doing distance healing, envision the individual (visualize them in your mind - or third eye) and send them the white light that was discussed before in the exercise for the crown chakra. Now, visualize this white light beginning at their feet and moving upward while round their body three times. The motion should be clockwise. The next step is to see the various hues of light associated with each chakra moving in a spiral around the person's chakras and then moving downward and upward along their body.

I have personally done this for members of my own family, loved ones, and friends, and they have all informed me that they felt more tranquil, joyful, and in charge of their life, as well as that they were better able to deal and cope with the circumstances that they were now in. You won't be able to deny the efficacy of ColorTherapy until you've experienced it for yourself and seen the changes it brings about in your life.

The methods of chakra-balancing color therapy are very efficient and result-oriented, so they may help you enhance all elements of your health, including the physical, mental, and spiritual components. You will eventually be able to go about your daily life with a beautifully soothing feeling of inner peace, stability, and happiness. This will allow you to live your life to the fullest. The fact that these procedures for balancing the chakras are offered without charge is another wonderful aspect of them. It is a free global gift that just needs you and your mind (or third eye), therefore there is no reason to believe that this is a business-formed hoax that promises it can sell happiness to you. So do yourself a favor and start seeing the colors around you!

ADDITIONAL METHODS FOR DETOXIFYING THE CHAKRAS

In a broad sense, the following kinds of activities may help clean and rebalance the seven chakras:

Reiki ()

The practice of qi gong yoga

Treatment with lithophane

Magnetic force

The study of sophrology

In addition to this, one of the best ways to keep them is to follow a balanced diet and engage in regular physical exercise.

Utilizing an internet magnetizer may assist you in clearing your chakras and bringing your energy back into balance.

You experience a significant decrease in energy, and you get disoriented. Or maybe you get the impression that you no longer have any influence or power over the events that occur in your life; any of these are indications that your energy needs to be cleaned up and rebalanced.

THE CHAPTER OF THE CHAKRAS as an Order

As can be seen, the primary chakras are given numbers between 1 and 7 that correspond to their relative positions. It is recommended that when we meditate, we begin with the seventh chakra, which is the crown chakra, and work our way down to the sixth chakra, and so on. There are many conceivable explanations for this arrangement, but only two of them are particularly straightforward.

To begin, we want energy to go from the head all the way down to the toes. The light travels from the top of the head down to the soles of the feet. This manner, rather than ending up stuck in our heads, we end up someplace else entirely.

Second, entering a profound trance state while practicing meditation makes it much simpler to descend. This induces an overwhelming sense of peace inside you.

HOW DO THE CHAKRAS ACTUALLY WORK

In traditional Indian medicine, which dates back more than 5,000 years, there is a belief that there are 88,000 chakras located throughout the human body. However, there are really seven primary chakras that run from the base of the spine to the crown of the head. As the energy flows from one chakra to the next, it generates an energy field all around the body of the individual. On the basis of the concept of communication vessels, they take in nourishment from the rest of the body and draw their strength from it. The existence of a chakra is evidence that we are alive and that we are receptive to the many experiences that life has to offer.

THE HEART CHAKRA'S IMPACT ON ANTISOCIAL BEHAVIOR AND ATTITUDES

The fourth chakra is the one that corresponds to the heart, and it is situated in the middle of the system of the seven chakras. It operates on feelings of compassion and love, as well as on our interactions with one another.

When the heart chakra is blocked, it may lead to antisocial conduct, which can tear a person away from their relationships and ultimately destroy them.

The exact translation is as follows:

"not struck" is the conventional translation of the Sanskrit word for the heart chakra, which is "Anahata."

It is simple to assume that when the energy in one's heart chakra is in harmony, they will experience more freedom and a greater willingness to connect with others. You will become "untouched" in a sense with regard to your social life. People are said to have antisocial tendencies if they do not wish to engage with other people, however this trait is not exclusive to them. You could have the impression that you are unable to engage with other people, that you are unable to form relationships, that you do not get the sense that others truly understand who you are, and that leads you to the conclusion that it is almost pointless to establish connections that will stay.

It's possible that your anxiety about other people and the quality of your relationships gets to the point that it seems like a weight. If this is how you have been feeling as of late, it may be the outcome of an issue that is deeper and more spiritual in nature.

The following are some possible symptoms of a blocked heart chakra:

Co-dependence is the need to seek the validation of others

Keeping a grudge and being unable to forgive someone

Create a mindset of helplessness in yourself.

Problems with responses

Heart illnesses caused by a lack of empathy

Being too judgmental of others

When your heart chakra is blocked, you may suffer various symptoms in addition to those stated above. It is crucial to keep in mind that these symptoms do not always manifest themselves when your heart chakra is congested.

It is also essential to provide proof that there are two clear extremes: either you will experience full isolation from other people, or you will become so reliant on the approval of other people that you will forget who you are in the process of trying to win their favor.

The following are some of the most significant aspects of the heart chakra:

Weeping or Mourning

Feelings of pity or sympathy

Discrimination motivated by compassion

a state of harmony and tranquility the capacity to love both oneself and others

Capacity for forgiving and accepting one's fellow humans

Establishment of links and associations between individuals

Awareism as well as fresh points of view

In its most basic form, the heart chakra is the doorway through which we may forge meaningful, long-lasting, and profound connections with the people in our lives. Because it is the chakra that brings together all of the other chakras' activities, it is the one that requires the greatest focus and care.

When the heart chakra is in harmony, all of the other chakras are, as well, and the result is a life that is full of vitality and contentment. If you want to rebalance the environment around you while the heart chakra is blocked, you need to be able to determine the cause of the blockage.

In order to purify your heart chakra and begin the process of emotional healing, you should make every effort to get rid of as many causes of stress as you possibly can in your life.

One of the most frequent ways to obstruct the flow of energy through your heart chakra and lead you down a perilous road is to refuse to let go of the emotional sorrow of the past. Discover how to let go in order to open yourself up.

The Seven Mantras That Purify

LAM is a cleaning mantra that is repeated for the Root Chakra. Chanting this mantra helps one remain rooted in the soil and connected to it. By chanting this mantra, impurities that have been held in the root chakra will be cleansed, which will actually open you up to emotions of security, prosperity, and belonging. Additionally, any blocked energy that has hindered a person from going upwards to the other six primary energy centers will also be cleared. Chant "LAM" if you feel like your energy is low, if you are having financial difficulties, if you have poor self-esteem, if you have adrenal exhaustion, or if you suffer from any other stress-related diseases.

VAM: This is a purifying mantra for the Sacral Chakra, which is connected to sexuality, pleasure, and creativity. The activation of this chakra will make you more receptive to other people, as well as offer you the confidence and bravery to express who you are and to welcome change. Chant "VAM" if you suffer from low libido, have a negative self-image, or find it difficult to be expressive in your interactions with people and family in general.

R.A.M. says that reciting this purifying mantra will open the Solar Plexus Chakra, which is the source of one's unique strength. Chanting "RAM" will strengthen your capacity to stand up for yourself, handle bad urges, and exhibit better self-control than you would otherwise have. As you continue to chant "RAM," you will see an increase in both your self-esteem and your level of self-assurance and confidence. If you suffer from regular stomach aches and worry, you will find that reciting this mantra helps reduce both of those symptoms.

YAM: The purification mantra for the Heart Chakra is as follows. Through the energy axis that is located in our heart chakra, we are able to both offer and receive love with one another. If we are not feeling loving, amicable, or sympathetic, or if we are going through a difficult time in our relationships, we might chant YAM! Chanting "YAM" heals both the physical heart as well as the spiritual (emotional) heart center, opens us up to unconditional love and compassion, and helps us open up to these feelings more fully.

HAM: The goal of this purifying mantra is to clear any obstructions from the Throat Chakra. This is both the physical and spiritual voice of our people, as well as the mechanism by which we communicate who we are and what we want from you and the universe. If we do not have the capacity to express ourselves, which comes from having a blocked throat chakra, we will discover that we are constantly irritated, which will cause us to shut ourselves off to opportunities and prevent us from getting our needs fulfilled. Additionally, having a closed throat chakra will make it difficult to demonstrate honesty and integrity. The vibrations from "RAM" will expand our throat chakra, allowing for a more powerful flow of energy associated with speech.

This purifying chant, referred to as AUM (or OM), awakens the Third Eye Chakra. This point is located in the middle of the forehead, just in the middle of the crease that separates the eyebrows. In spite of the fact that OM is one of the most well-known mantras and that it is used extensively during mantra meditations, it is of utmost significance for the purpose of purifying and repairing the third eye chakra. The third eye chakra is where one's intuition and sense of life's purpose are magnified. By not letting oneself to listen to their own inner knowledge and using that insight to design the best route for a life of purpose and passion, a person may have unintentionally put some limitations upon themselves. Chanting "OM" will help a person break free from these limitations and set them free.

These purifying mantras, such as OM or AH, are for the Crown Chakra, which is the connection to the divine. Feelings of insignificance and worthlessness are brought on by an obstruction in the crown chakra, which in turn leads to a detachment from the spirit realm and an unhealthy preoccupation with material goods, interpersonal connections, and the external world. OM is one method that may be utilized to open the crown chakra, although other people believe that silence is a more beneficial practice for opening the crown chakra. A release is indicated by chanting the letter 'AH'. Imagine drawing a full breath in and then letting it out all at once. The sound of letting go and surrendering oneself is represented by the letter AH.

The Sacral Chakra Is Located In The Lower Abdomen.

The orange hue in the rainbow spectrum corresponds to the sacral chakra, which may be found around one to two inches below your naval and is positioned in the lower part of your body. Ovaries, testicles, genital organs, the womb, kidneys, pancreas, and adrenal glands are all connected to this condition. The sacral chakra is the place where sexual energy, unfiltered emotions, and creative expression are focused.

This chakra absorbs oxygen directly from the air, turns it into energy, and then uses that energy to facilitate spiritual awareness, sexuality, integration, and creative expression. In addition to this, it is founded on the concepts of power and raw energy and is related with water.

You will typically have a great deal of sexual energy, power, and healing energy while it is open. In addition to this, you have a high degree of creative ability and focus mostly on artistic pursuits. However, if the chakra located in your lower belly is blocked, your sexual experience will be weak, you will feel dissatisfied, and at times you may struggle with poor self-esteem. This is because your sexual energy will be obstructed.

It's possible that your second chakra is out of whack if you struggle with feelings of guilt. If it is out of balance, you are also likely to have difficulties with money, in which you feel unworthy of spending money on yourself. If it is out of balance, it is probable that you will have both of these problems. On the other side, if this chakra is hyperactive, the effect may be uncontrolled sexual energy with a lot of concentration on material things. This is because this chakra is located in the sacral region of the body. Other negative repercussions of the lower abdominal chakra include sexual issues, the desire to possess, overindulging in food, feelings of jealously and envy, and perplexity.

When it is in a state of harmony, this chakra is related with positive characteristics as well. A few excellent examples are working well with people, having tolerance, being open to new ideas, giving and receiving love passionately, and giving and getting gifts.

3. The Chakra of the Solar Plexus

This chakra may be found at the middle of the body, just below the sternum and directly above the navel. In the range of colors that make up the rainbow, it is denoted by the yellow hue. It is connected to the gastrointestinal tract, the liver, the pancreas, and the neurological system, as well as the muscles. Because it is connected to things like your own willpower, integrity, intention, and metabolic energy, it plays a very significant part in the functioning of your body.

Your urges and impulses are brought to you via the solar plexus chakra, and your emotions are under its control. It is also connected to the element of fire, and it serves as the basis of your personality. As the basis of your personality, it determines your responses and the emotions that you experience, such as happiness or despair.

When the solar plexus chakra is open and balanced, it brings with it a feeling of wellbeing, tranquility, and tenderness, as well as a tremendous emotional power. When everything is in check, it bolsters your strength by providing you with personal inspiration. When it is out of whack, it has the potential to generate undesirable ideas and behaviours. If this pathway is blocked, it may also contribute to panic episodes. You can have a persistent feeling of insecurity and weakness and be easily bullied into not making your own choices.

Pancreatitis, adrenal difficulties, hepatitis, intestinal disorders, duodenal ulcers, diabetes, liver malfunction, and arthritis are some of the medical issues that are linked to this chakra.

Trust, fear, self-confidence, self-care, intimidation, responsibilities in decision making, sensitive to personal honor and self esteem are some of the emotional and spiritual concerns associated with the solar plexus chakra. The qualities associated with this chakra include authority, self control, mastery of desire, personal power, immortality, humor, laughter, and radiance.

4. The Chakra of the Heart

The location of the heart chakra is in the middle of the chest, about two to three inches higher than the solar plexus. In the range of colors that make up the rainbow, it is denoted by the color green. The heart, the glands, the arms, the circulatory system, the lungs, the breast, the ribs, and the diaphragm are the bodily organs that are connected with the heart chakra.

The love and compassion that are at the core of our being are housed in the heart chakra. In addition to this, it is associated with feelings such as contentment, reverence, honesty, generosity, and pleasure. This is the reason why, in a lot of different cultures, the heart is considered to be the mother of all of us as well as the place where the soul resides. Additionally, the sensation of connection with other people is brought about through the heart chakra.

When the heart chakra is activated, it serves as a conduit for the flow of unconditional love, and the qualities associated with having a good heart are distributed throughout the whole body. In addition to this, it replaces your anxieties with compassion in the form of spiritual love, which is an essential instrument that brings about wholeness. In addition to this, it plays a significant part in the spiritual healing process.

On the other side, if your heart chakra is blocked, you will feel an inadequate flow of emotional sustenance and love. As a result, you will be more likely to experience unpleasant emotions such as egotism, impatience, guilt, hate, and a variety of other feelings.

Because your heart chakra is blocked, you won't be able to experience love for other people, and your relationship with yourself will become unhealthy and narcissistic. It is possible that you will spend your whole life carrying a great deal of stress in each and every region of your body. The bitterness and rage that are stuffed deep inside your heart will, in due time, accumulate to the point where they will emerge as an illness.

5. The Chakra of the Throat

This is the mother chakra, and it is associated with creative expression, expressing oneself authentically, and even communication. The throat chakra is responsible for the control of one's ability to communicate verbally. This chakra is associated with clairaudience, which refers to one's capacity to pick up on the tones and vibrations of spiritual communication, as well as with the element of sound. This chakra is also involved with the process of reception, which might include things like music, language, sounds, scents, and taste.

The solar plexus sends ideas to the throat chakra, commonly known as our voice, and the throat chakra relays those thoughts in a manner that is more tangible. The body's throat chakra is activated to produce feelings of love, joy, and serenity when it is working in conjunction with the heart chakra.

In most cases, our life experiences are immediately translated into our ideas, after which they are changed into words, and finally, they are translated into deeds with the assistance of this chakra, which directs and focuses our thoughts into language. The tremendous power that our voice possesses has the capacity to change our desires and intentions, and even to help us bring our dreams to life.

When the throat chakra is opened, the divine will is brought into harmony, which results in a deep awareness of the purpose of life and the cosmos as well as a feeling of liberation.

The opening of this chakra, together with the proper functioning of sound, makes it possible to embrace others with love and warmth. It helps you feel safe in your own expression, which ultimately leads to you making choices that are more transparent, which in turn makes it simpler for you to achieve the objectives you have set for yourself in life without any reservations.

A lack of willpower and drive might be a symptom of the throat chakra being blocked. It causes feelings of powerlessness and inadequacy, which, along with the fact that it is difficult to articulate one's emotions and ideas, may become a burden. Some individuals develop eating disorders such as bulimia and anorexia nervosa as a consequence of bottling up their emotions within. Others generate a lot of conflict because they are quick to anger and don't give much consideration to the consequences of their actions before they leap into a situation.

6. The Chakra of the Third Eye

This chakra is connected to one's innate abilities as well as their imagination and perception. It makes use of the quality of light and functions as the energetic core from which you are able to access higher spiritual levels. Because it enables you to perceive all of the conditions in your environment, the third eye is considered to be the doorway to knowledge, wisdom, and the truth.

When one is meditating, dreaming, or manipulating the energy of the chakra, the third eye contributes to the process of bringing out inner knowledge in the form of visuals, colors, and sensations. This energy center is the ultimate power center for healing ourselves as well as others and having a better grasp of the world around us since it gives us the capacity to comprehend mental ideas and the ability to envision them.

When your third eye is opened and in a balanced state, you will see significant improvements in the areas of creativity, imagination, and instinct. Because of the third eye, it's possible that you'll start to feel or know things that aren't as well developed.

If this chakra has grown more in this center than the others have, you may find that it is difficult for you to deal with things relating to everyday routines and even bodily concerns. If this chakra is powerful but dysfunctional, you may find yourself caught up in illusions and glamour, and you may even find yourself drawn to drugs in the hope that they may briefly offer you access to the world of your dreams.

It is possible that if this energy center is shut off, it will lead to a lack of creativity, a confined imagination, and a lesser degree of consciousness; as a result, one's life will be of a poorer quality in terms of higher direction. People who have issues with their third eye often do not believe in anything that cannot be seen or proven in a tangible way. They find it difficult to be religious, and as a consequence, the great majority of them do not believe in God or in life after death. They also do not think that there is life after death. They have an unshakable confidence in concepts such as scientific knowledge, interpretations at the surface level, and their own intellectual competence.

7. The chakra located in the third eye

It is stated that this chakra is the connection that links the physical body to the spiritual world. It is located in the groin area. It is the basis upon which all other forms of information, knowledge, and cognition are constructed. It is related to the pineal gland, which is engaged in the administration of the internal click of the body; as a consequence, it is connected with thoughts. The internal click of the body is managed by the pineal gland.

According to the teachings of Eastern mysticism, after a direct connection has been made with a higher self, the crown chakra is considered to be the origin of respect, infinity, or knowledge, as well as an insight that originates from a spiritual comprehension. This occurs when the third eye chakra has been opened. By connecting to a consciousness that exists beyond your own self and the physical world, you may go to other energy realities such as the sky by using this energy center. This awareness exists beyond both the physical world and your own individual self. Through the employment of it, it is even possible that you may be able to receive guidance or other knowledge from a superior life.

The realizations that one attains are the wellspring from which one draws their brilliant intellect, profound religious experience, and exceptional intuitive capacity. If you activate your crown chakra, you have the ability to be able to send healing, unconditional love, and energy to every area in the cosmos. This chakra provides the base for the spiritual power of prayer and energy healing therapies such as therapeutic touch and Reiki. It also symbolizes the foundation of the chakra system. The crown chakra is connected with a variety of concepts, including grace, angels, immorality, and the capacity to communicate with the spirits of the heavens.

Once you have a better understanding of chakras, the next step is to learn how to balance, cleanse, and repair your own chakras. This is a very important step. One method for accomplishing this goal is to meditate on various hues.

The use of music is essential in order to restore health to the chest and heart region.

Begin by selecting a tune with a soothing melody, one that has pleasant rhythms and noises but no words, since this will prevent you from singing along in your brain.

It has been shown via research that listening to the proper kind of music may improve one's mood, thus it is important to look for songs or albums to which one can feel an emotional connection.

Turn it on by a few bars so that it is audible but not too loud, for example, by turning it on at one-fourth of the way through the music bars.

Be sure that the song lasts for at least 10 minutes, or play it again and over again.

First, choose a comfortable position to lie down in and let yourself to unwind.

If you want the maximum amount of comfort, put a cushion under your head and another one under your legs.

Place your palms facing up next to your body while your hands are laying down close to your body.

Take a moment to bring your attention within and clear your thoughts by taking several deep breaths.

Take a deep breath in via your nose, pause for two seconds while holding it, and then exhale through your mouth.

Keep using this simple and easy breathing method for the next minute.

While you focus on relaxing your body as much as you can while you inhale through your nose and exhale through your mouth, you should try to relax your body as much as you can.

The next step is to slowly close your eyes while directing all of your focus on the region around your chest.

When you breathe, breathe out through your chest rather than through your stomach.

This indicates that when you take a breath in, you should give your lungs room to expand so that they may begin to move around and fill with oxygen.

Make sure that you are focusing all of your attention on your chest, specifically how it expands and contracts as you breathe in and out, as well as how the rest of your body either becomes larger as you breathe in or becomes smaller as you breathe out.

Imagine that with each breath you take, you are able to release any tensions or pollutants that have built up in your chest, releasing them via your lips and enabling yourself to let go of any impurities or tensions that have built up.

As you continue to let your body relax and as you grow more used to the rhythm of your body's deep breathing, start paying close attention to the many melodies that you hear and make an effort to zero in on one in particular that sticks out to you. This will help you to concentrate on the one that is most important to you.

For instance, if the sound of the bells is what you are concentrating on, then draw your attention on those bells.

While you listen to that calm and soothing music, you should make an effort to push any thoughts that may be arising to the back of your brain and instead focus on relaxing.

Take a minute to savor the sound of the music that you are now listening to.

Consider how this tune makes you feel on an emotional level. Are you experiencing joy and love in your heart? If yes, continue by imagining your heart beating faster and faster, as if it were becoming more receptive to love.

Imagine that your heart is a flower whose petals are opening out and floating all around you, waiting to be sent out to your loved ones.

Maintain contact with your own experience of love, and link that experience to the petals of the flower.

Think of a person who is important to you, such as a friend, a lover, or a member of your family, and imagine sending them dazzling pink or green petals, full with the love and compassion that you feel for them.

I hope they are blessed with joy and success throughout their lives.

Imagine those petals moving to wherever they are at the moment and making contact with their hearts as they do so.

Participate in this activity with two or three additional individuals who have a special place in your heart.

Feel the warmth and tingle as more petals emerge from your heart and make their way to the people you care about.

Allow the energy that has been building up in your heart to flow out into the rest of your body; while you do so, feel love spreading throughout your whole being.

Allow the energy to flow freely up and down your spine via all of your chakras, bringing them together and fostering your development on a spiritual level.

Step one is to set your purpose to bring the energy back to the surface, and step two is to consult the cosmos for direction on this exercise.

Keep your concentration on the white auric field that encircles your body and helps you to feel secure and at ease.

You will start to experience tingling sensations all over your body, along with a warm feeling.

Allow the healing energy to slowly resurface throughout your body and allow it to focus on the location of your heart. This will help it to work more effectively.

As you continued to do the exercise of releasing petals, your heart got more cheerful and pure, which made it simpler for the energy to enter and move through it.

Put forth the desire to be protected against everything unfavorable that may occur in your life, including unfavorable experiences, unfavorable feelings, and unfavorable individuals.

Because of this, you will feel more protected and at peace in the face of adversity.

Set another intention with the goal of getting self-healing energy, this time focusing on the chest area of your body.

Permit that energy to go from your heart to your shoulders and then down to the palms of your hands, all the while maintaining a connection with one another while it does so.

You should direct your energy onto your hands and focus on using them as a focal point for it.

It is important that you allow the flow of white energy to reappear in your hands so that they may radiate a pure white tone.

Spend a moment simply allowing all of the energy to catch up and collect in one location, and in the process, heal the hands as it works its way through the body.

Raise both of your hands to your chest and rest them there, overlapping one on top of the other.

Permit the energy to flow into your heart chakra, and in your mind's eye, see the white light transform into the vibrant green hue that is linked with the heart chakra.

Put your attention on feeling the beat of your heart against your palms, and focus on sensing the pulsating sensations that are occurring below.

Take a deep breath and try to relax as you feel the green light go deeper into your chest.

Permit the energy to go freely around the chest region and investigate it, directing it to go precisely where tension is present.

Feel the tingling sensations all over your body, smell the air around you as you take in deep breaths, hear the soft melody echoing in the room or against your ears, taste the freedom and love that life gives you, and finally, notice the glowing green light emerging through your heart even though your eyes are closed.

Imagine that the color is shining more brightly as it awakens your heart chakra to all of the love and happiness that you rightfully deserve.

Think back on the many occasions on which love was shown to you and given to you; remember that even the little things that brought you joy still matter.

Make room in your heart for the mending that you need.

To assist you in opening this chakra even more, use the mantra "yam."

Invest some time into opening your chakra; don't try to hurry through the process; instead, give your body the time it needs to mend its heart, whether that be emotionally or physically.

To finish, take several minutes to concentrate only on the music and the range of sensations that it elicits in you as you take slow, deep breaths in through your mouth and out through your nose.

The purpose of this meditation is to fill your chest region with good and unadulterated energy while also making you experience love for life, love for others around you, and most importantly, love for yourself.

When you reach the point where you believe you are done, stop what you are doing and let the energy settle into your body for a minute or two.

Allow your eyes to gradually acclimate to the light and the environment around you as you allow them to open gradually.

Be sure to give some thought to the healing that has come to you as a result of the meditation that you have just finished doing.

Step one is to get started by engaging in an activity that brings you pleasure or that you like.

After the healing process is complete, you should give yourself permission to rest and not rush into doing anything.

Stay in, take it easy, soak in a warm bath, and give your body time to mend itself while the energy that is still inside it.

www.ingramcontent.com/pod-product-compliance
Lightning Source LLC
Chambersburg PA
CBHW052134110526
44591CB00012B/1712